PEGGY'S SCRAPBOOK

Lucas Books

PEGGY'S SCRAPBOOK

Growing Flowers and Vegetables and How to Show Them
by Peggy Cole

First Published by LUCAS BOOKS 2006
ISBN 1903797-54-3
EAN 9781903797549

Copyright Peggy Cole 2006

Printed in the UK by Winsor Clarke Brackenbury Ltd

CONTENTS

GARDEN HINTS

Gardening lore has been passed down the generations ever since the Egyptians cultivated exotic plants gathered from all over Europe. This has continued to happen to us with tips passed down by our fathers, mothers and grandparents and we say the old tips are the best and still work today.

Apples

Do not store autumn apples and winter apples together, as autumn apples give off a gas that will hasten the ripening of winter apples and may cause them to rot.

Asparagus

I am often asked when you should stop cutting asparagus. I have always been told on the longest day, which is June 21st. While I am writing about the longest day, my father always used to take shallots up on this day and tried to plant them on the shortest day, December 21st.

Bees swarming on hot days can be made to settle by making a loud noise. My brother would bang on a dustbin lid and it worked every time, so I know this is right. Bee stings are said to be a cure for arthritis and rheumatism (nettle tea is also said to help rheumatism) Common soda can ease bee stings.

Cabbage
Sow spring cabbage in late July and plant out in the autumn into unmanured ground. Sow both winter and summer cabbages in March and sow winter cabbage again in early May for succession.

Charcoal. Add a little charcoal when planting in pots to keep the water sweet.

Clean Hands
To clean your hands after gardening or doing the flowers, rub them with a mixture of lemon juice, a little sugar and olive oil. This is very successful.

Clematis
Remember to plant clematis with their heads in the sun and roots in the shade.

Comfrey

I used to grow this herb as it had so many uses. You can eat it like spinach and it makes a good feed for plants by soaking the leaves in a bucket of water. Leave for a few days then dilute and use a half-comfrey to half-water mix. Also I swear by comfrey hand lotion for dry skin. It is known as the healing herb as it has so many uses, such as for sprains, poultices, bruises and swellings.

Cut shrubs

Bring flowering shrubs into the house while still tightly in bud. Cut small branches, hammering the stems and stand them in warm water. Standing them in an airing cupboard will make them open earlier still.

Deadheading

This is so important. You will notice this in sweet peas. If you leave the seedpods on you will soon lose your blooms. If you have the time, walk round the garden each day and do your deadheading.

Dandelion Leaves
These can be made into salads and the roots used to make coffee and also beer and wine. Caged birds love the seeds and the leaves were given to caged rabbits, particularly from April to September when they are breeding.

Dark and Light
Keep potatoes in the dark and onions in the light to prevent them sprouting when stored. Apples are best stored in the cellar where it is cool and pears in the attic where air rises. But keep a hawk's eye on both these fruits to catch them at the right moment for eating.

Elderflower infusion makes a good anti-catterpillar spray. Boil about 10-12 heads in 2 litres (1/2 Gallon) of water, allow to cool then strain. Add a few drops of washing-up liquid to aid sticking to leaves.

Fat Hen

This weed will grow very well on poor soil but it is a wonderful vegetable used in salad or made into tarts. I have used it with cheese and mushrooms. You cook it like broccoli. Once cooked it goes down in size like spinach but it is worthwhile so if it grows in your garden don't throw it away, use it. It is also a good poultry food and caged birds like the seed heads.

Flowers

To keep cut flowers fresh, cut and split the stalks a little every day or as often as possible. Add a pinch of salt and soda to the water.

Fuchsias. I use to grow a lot of Fushsias and soon learnt that they do not like the full sun. People often give me cuttings. I fit a foil top over a jam jar, half filled with water. Make a small hole in the foil and push the cutting through the hole into the water to form roots before planting out.

Garlic

Plant a few bulbs among roses to help strengthen the bushes' resistance to disease. I have also heard that if you plant garlic or leeks between rows of strawberries, it helps protect the fruit from grey mould.

Geranium cuttings are best taken in July and August if you want them to flower next summer. This is a better time than the spring.

Golden Wedding Presents

So often we don't know what present to give for an occasion such as this. Why not offer fifty yellow roses or a few "Golden Wedding" rose bushes? The same idea can be used for a Silver Wedding – twenty-five roses or, again, the "Silver Wedding" bushes to plant in the garden.

If you have had a rosebud for a wedding buttonhole, prolong its life by singeing it with a flame then placing it in a small vase with old-fashioned fizzy lemonade. It will stay fresh for a few days.

Good Neighbours for your Plants
You will see pictures in books of cottage gardens of many years ago with vegetables and flowers all mixed up in rows. This is how they found out how one crop would help another. It also helped in discovering more about pests and diseases.
If you want a bumper crop of broccoli, the companion plant is spinach. The roots of the spinach secrete a growth-enhancing hormone into the soil, which does wonders for the many vegetables grown nearby.
Plant caraway in your potato patch to enhance their flavour.
Savory has a smell that deters black bean aphids.

Ground Elder
We all have to get this weed out of our gardens. I find the best way is to cover the area with an old carpet and leave for 12-18 months. No weedkiller seems to kill it off.

Hawthorn

I remember that as we walked to school we used to pick the tender shoots to eat, calling it "bread and cheese". I have picked the berries and made jelly and also homemade wine. Even the flowers produce a light wine. I can also remember that if we got a splinter in our fingers a handful of young hawthorn leaves would be boiled in water for 2 to 3 minutes. These were drained and put between two pieces of rag, which were placed on the splinter. The heat from the leaves would dry the splinter.

Holly branches, or twigs from Gorse or other really prickly shrubs can be used to protect newly sown seed from birds and mice. Spread the branches flat over the drills and anchor down with small stakes.

House plants

Always use soft water if you can as most tap water contains so much lime. This then turns to alkaline and blooms don't like this. Azaleas, for one, will soon go brown.

Also water your plants with leftover tea. They will benefit from the boiled water and the fact that it's more likely to be tepid than stone cold, which chills plants.
Keep houseplants away from oil heaters and gas appliances. Also plants don't like smoke so if you are expecting a group of smoking guests remove your plants.

No plant likes a big change in temperature from day to night. That's why I don't like to see plants outside shops in all weathers. Buy from a good nursery.

Plants breathe through their leaves so they need to be clean. Wipe large leaves on both sides with a damp cloth or moistened cotton wool. Clean soft, hairy leaves with a small artist's brush.
Plants with this kind of leaf should not get wet .

Encourage further blooming of pot plants by removing flowers as soon as they are dead and thus preventing seeds forming.

To prevent plants growing too large, keep them in small pots and repot only when the pots are plainly full of roots.

Never use detergent or oil on plant leaves to make them glossy as this will damage the surface. Water does the trick satisfactorily.

If you think you've over watered a plant, stand the pot on several thicknesses of newspaper so that excess water can be drawn from the roots. Let it become very nearly dry at the roots before watering it again. Also use soft rainwater for pot plants. You can stand them outside in rain in summer months.

Hydrangeas
One question I am often asked is why hydrangeas won't turn blue. On acid soils they will turn blue but if you had a pink one and want to change it to blue, add aluminium sulphate to the soil and the old fashioned way was to plant rusty nails or copper wire near to the roots.

Manure
Use cow or pig manure on light soils and horse manure to lighten heavy soils. Cover fresh manure heaps while they rot down to prevent evaporation and dilution by rain.

Marigolds
For as long as I can remember, many people have planted French marigolds to keep white fly off tomatoes or chrysanthemums. It's not totally effective but it will help.

Herbs
Most people with small gardens will have to grow a few herbs. Remember that flat-leaf parsley is more aromatic than the curly-leaf variety. Both make attractive garnishes. Use fennel, dill, marigold and nasturtium flowers as attractive garnishes on summer salads.
Smaller herb varieties such as basil, thyme, chives or parsley are ideal for planting in window boxes. Savory seeds need light to germinate. Sow under a thin covering of soil.

Mulberry trees
Did you know the mulberry is called the wise tree because it never shows a leaf until all danger of frost is past?

The Medlar tree is another tree that is believed to bring happiness to the owner in whose garden it grows. When my father used to talk about medlars, I thought he was saying, "don't medlar about". It's an odd looking fruit. You eat it once picked and left to "blet", in other words to decay. Then you scoop out the middle contents and eat with a spoon. You can also make jelly or jam with them. You pick them in November and they look like very large brown coloured rosehips.

Mint
Flies and mosquitoes hate mint. Rub a fresh sprig on your exposed parts before working in the garden.

Nettles
We know the butterflies love them but they do make good soup and beer too. For arthritis and rheumatism eat regularly and drink nettle tea. The medicinal books list a number of nettle cures.

Onions
I always used to sow onions in my greenhouse on Boxing Day and also a few broad beans in pots. Both like a long growing time.

Parsley
This is a herb I love to grow. Some people like to put boiling water in a drill before sowing but I like to soak seed in hot water then sow it in a seed tray in the greenhouse. It will soon come up and then you can prick it out into pots. The plant is also said to grow better when seeds are sown by a woman!

Pears
This fruit develops its full flavour when at room temperature. If pears are for immediate eating, avoid storing them in a cold place.

Potatoes
Potatoes always used to be planted on Good Friday. But Easter is a movable feast; it falls on the first Sunday after the first full moon following the vernal equinox, 21st March.

Quinces
I find a lot of people don't know what these are. No one ever forgets seeing a quince tree for the first time when branches bow down almost to the ground with the weight of huge fruit. They are the legend of love. A single quince will perfume an entire room and just a spoonful of quince conserve added to any apple dish will transform it into food of the gods. I love making quinces into jelly and eating it with meats. Christmas would not be the same without quince jelly and turkey.

Roses.
Remember to prune weak plants harder than robust ones. Also prune newly planted roses hard. You won't hurt them!
Most gardens have rose bushes. I wonder do you ever collect the rosehips? I expect you remember when boys would split them open when you were in school and put them down your back! But what a wonderful fruit. You can use them to make jellies, jams and wines. And think how good they were in the Second World War as they were made into rosehip syrup for our young babies because they are so full of vitamin C. The syrup was given to keep the children healthy.

Rust
Keep small garden tools rust free by storing them in a bucket of oiled sand. Also at the end of the year give all garden tools a good clean with an oily rag.

Samphire

Marsh samphire is a fine vegetable and only has a short season. Don't pick after the end of July as it gets too tough. It's best cut with scissors. Wash well to get the salty water off the plants. Never soak it as it soon decays. It will keep unwashed and quite dry in a plastic bag in the bottom of the refrigerator for three days. I have pickled it, as it will keep longer this way.

Storing Bulbs

Some people dig up their garden bulbs and store them over the winter. Others leave them in the ground and hope they will multiply. I dig a small trench and line it with some chicken netting, place my bulbs in the netting and cover them. You can lift the netting out in the autumn and your bulbs will be ready for planting.

Sweet pea

Another seed that likes a long growing time is the sweet pea. You put some seed in during October, out in the garden to stand the winter. You will soon see how strong the plants are in the spring!

Seeds

My dad used to save all his own seeds and I thought this little tale would help you:

Have in your drawer since Candlemas day, all seed packets you daren't throw away.

Throw out the parsnip, they're no good next year, unlike all the cabbage family, broccoli, cauliflower, sprouts and kale, some of which last for three years or perhaps even four or five. Kohl rabi will also last the same. Turnips and swedes have a short life of just one year. You can buy half a pound of mustard and cress as this will last. Radish lasts four years and lettuce seed will last three more years. Beetroot and spinach beet will last for four years but ordinary spinach is best within one year. Leeks only last three years but onion seed will keep for four years or more. With carrots it is best to use fresh seed each year. Now, marrow and cucumbers you can save for seven years. Celery is another seed that you can keep for six years. With broad beans, French and runner beans, some can go on for years. If you have a good one, take care and save them. Peas will keep for two or three years but you do have to watch that

maggots don't start to eat the seeds. Do store the seeds in a tin. Plastic will not do as they get damp and also mice will eat into the plastic.
Try using fibre trays to raise seedlings instead of the more expensive peat pots. They will rot in the ground in exactly the same way. This avoids disturbing the roots.

Slugs

Slugs are a problem in some gardens. The best way to get rid of them was to put barley chaff or old soot down but you can't find them today. They don't like gravel so put this round the tops of your pots. Also put a good smear of Vaseline round the tops of pots on the outer brim. Save old eggshells to put round hostas.

Tools

Come in many different weights and sizes as well as prices. The cheapest is not always the best. Choose secateurs that fit your hand. Is the spade too big or heavy? Lift the handle and try equipment if possible. Small local suppliers are normally happy to give you help and advice.

Old Tights

So many uses can be found for old tights around the garden. You can use them for storing bulbs and also onions. Just hang them up in a cool, dry place. Stockings and tights, cut into strips, will make useful ties in the garden and greenhouse. The stretch in them won't restrict growth. I have also used old rubber gloves by cutting strips from the fingers.

Tomatoes, good and bad

Old gardeners uproot tomato plants at the end of the season and hang them on boughs of fruit trees to wither. This is supposed to prevent disease and blight. Sometimes they burn the old plants under the apple trees so that the smoke rising among the branches will destroy insects and blight. Anyone who is prone to attacks of gout should never eat tomatoes.

Watercress

We used to love to pick this out of the streams, as watercress will only grow in clear running water in the wild. I love the soup that can be made from this wild plant but you do have a job to find it these days. It's very good if you suffer from anaemia so eat plenty of salads. It also gives you a clear complexion and healthy hair.

A Good Weeder

Drive two nails into the end of an old broomstick. Use this by sinking the nails into the ground over the centre of a weed and giving a cunning twist. The weed will lift out and your back will not ache at the end of the day.

Wild Hops

We all know these are used by the brewer but I love to see them on display at harvest festivals in church. If you have indigestion, take one cupful of hops and infuse in hot water. Strain and drink three times a day.

Waste not want not
This has always been my motto and when I had a large garden all my kitchen refuse used to go on the compost heap (not potato peelings as they grow. I used to boil them up for the chickens, mixing them with meal. The chickens loved them). Tea leaves were put round the camellias. They seemed to benefit from them.

When you put milk bottles out, rinse the milky liquid and tip it on your climbers or hanging baskets. Before the days of detergents, soapy water was used for cabbages in particular. My father used to empty the old copper after the clothes had been boiled in it. This was put into buckets and it used to set like a jelly but he loved it for his vegetables.

SHOWS

If you are a show person, this will help you.

VEGETABLES

Broad Beans
These offer very little scope, so all you can do is cut with scissors and try to arrange neatly. Too often people just put them on the table, stick a number on them and leave them.

Brussels Sprouts
Here a uniform size is required. Do not remove too many outer leaves otherwise the depth of colour is reduced.

Cabbages
These should be clean and have good hard centres.

Carrots
Leave these till last. Lift them and wash only with cold water, keeping the foliage, then put them in a damp cloth. The top of the carrot should not have green on it; this is caused by exposure when growing, so cover the soil as they grow to prevent this. Carrots soon lose their colour if left in the light.

Cauliflowers
They must be white, not yellowy and certainly not brown. If a cauliflower looks good in the week before the show, pick off the outside leaves and lay them over the top of the cauliflower to keep its colour.

Celery
I don't show this for the simple reason that we can't grow good enough specimens for show purposes. On our soil, the slugs always get to the celery before we do! But if you are showing, then tie each specimen below the foliage and lie it flat on the bench.

Cucumbers

Try to get completely matched pairs, with a nice dark colour and blossoms still attached. Again lie flat on the bench to display.

Collection Tray

Try to arrange your collection in order of points:

e.g.

Potatoes	20 points
Runner beans	15 points
Tomatoes	20 points
Parsnips	20 points
Onions	20 points
Cauliflowers	20 points
Peas	20 points
Leeks	20 points
Celery	20 points
Carrots	20 points
Cucumber	18 points

French beans and Runner beans
First pick with scissors, then wrap in damp paper. I then wrap mine in an old damp cloth, which helps to keep them straight. Sometimes, if you do it carefully, it is possible to bend a bean straight. Of course, the most important thing is to make sure the beans are young ones.

Lettuces
Like cabbages, they should be clean with a good centre. Lift with the root on and wash and wrap the root with a damp cloth and pop it all in a bag to keep the root damp.

Marrows
These do bruise easily, so take care how you pack for the show. You should display a matching pair.

Onions
This is one of my favourite vegetables for showing. I don't know why, but so many people spoil their exhibits by peeling off all the outside skins. This should never be done. Again, take the trouble to arrange your exhibit nicely on the stand.

Peas
These should be picked off with scissors in order not to damage the calyx and do try to leave the waxy bloom on the pea. I always hold mine up to the light to check how many peas are in the pods and to see if there are any maggots!

Potatoes
Wash each one carefully with a sponge dipped in a little milk. Put under a wet cloth, then when dry wrap in tissue paper and keep under several layers of newspapers, making sure that you don't let the daylight get to them as this quickly turns them green.

Red Beet
Globe beet will develop two weeks before long beet. Be careful when lifting not to break the taproot as this will lead to bleeding and will lose you marks on the show bench. Wash the beet in cold water and trim the side roots carefully. Pack in a damp cloth. Remember to leave the top leaves on.

Shallots
Here is something you can prepare in advance. They should all be of an even size and tied down at the neck to look like miniature onions. They look best if you can stand them in a pot of sand.

Tomatoes
Always show with the calyx left on.

FLOWER ARRANGING AND JUDGING

This is a lovely art, creating our own designs out of nature's beauty and essentially it is something you do for sheer pleasure. However, many shows do have a class for flower arrangements and as I both enter and act as a judge, I will pass on a few of the principles used in judging.

Interpretation of the Schedule
This needs very careful thought. For instance, if the class is for an 'Arrangement for Welcome', you would need to use nice bright flowers, yellows and reds, not mauves and greys. The dark colours, however attractive the flowers may be, are not cheerful or warm.

Design

This is very important. A good design has a good pattern and balance. You need to make sure that the smaller flowers, which are more graceful, are at the top of the design and the larger are lower down the scale.

Scale

This means that the flowers in the arrangement must be in scale with the vase or container. Many really beautiful arrangements have been spoilt by the vase being too big or too small or even the wrong shape for the arrangement.

Azaleas

Submerge the pot in a bucket of rain water once a week until the bubbles have subsided. Drain well before returning the plant. This should stop the azalea from flagging. Rain water is always best!

Balance
If you were to draw an imaginary line through the centre of the arrangement, each side would appear a visually equal balance.

Colour
As you judge an arrangement, you have to decide for yourself if the colour in the flower or plant material used in the design fully interprets what is asked for by the schedule.

Suitability of Container
In colour, texture and harmony, the container should suit the material it holds. A base is considered part of the container providing it holds a water-retaining receptacle about it. This could be a small tin or dish (I have used old polish tins and even an old sugar basin) but once it has been hidden it will be the base which is in colour, texture or size with the flowers used. If your design is meant to suggest something of a bygone age then you would try to use a period piece as a container, while a modern design demands large

Condition of Plant Material

There is nothing more likely to spoil an arrangement than 'droopy' foliage. Make sure your flowers have a good drink apply here.

Berries

When using berries, to make them last longer, put a dessertspoon of glycerine into a pint of water and bring to the boil. Stand the stems in a metal container and pour the boiling mixture over the stems to a depth of 2-3 inches. Leave for 24 hours before arranging in fresh water. This does not preserve the berries, it simply extends their life.

Distinction and Quality

When you are judging an arrangement this is the most difficult part to define. I look for some original thought, which might include the use of drapes – a piece of cloth behind an arrangement helps to give it colour and height – or the unusual placement of different sized bases.

One final word, do make sure that if you have wired any of your plant material, the wire does not show. These are tips for shows but the important thing to remember is that God gave us flowers to enjoy whether they are growing in the garden or beautifully arranged in a vase. And what mother hasn't been moved by the present of a bunch of Buttercups crammed into a jam jar or made into a picture at school and lovingly brought home for Mothering Sunday? I often make flower pictures to give as presents or for sale at fund-raising bazaars.

Forsythia

picked in late December and brought indoors will come into flower early in the house. The stems can be used as light stakes for indoor bulbs.

Leaves

Beech, oak and Hawthorn leaves as well as ferns can be pressed dry, there by keeping them green. Simply arrange them carefully between plenty of newspaper and put them under the rug. Leave them for about 8 weeks before arranging them.

Mint

For an early crop, lift a few runners in January, bring indoors and lay flat in a pot of compost about 1 inch below the surface. Water well and keep on the kitchen window sill.

Poppies

Use a candle flame or gas lighter to singe the stems of poppies to extend the life of the cut flowers.

Rust

When using crumpled wire to arrange flowers use a pinch of Borax in the water to prevent it rusting and discolouring the ware

Tea!

Water your kitchen plants with cold left-over tea. Coffee grounds, and tea leaves are excellent for mixing with the soil in flowerpots. This is particularly good for ferns.

Violets

African Violets can be encouraged to bloom by feeding with tomato fertilizer. Their should also be kept in a small pot.

Watering

Before watering stick a pencil into the soil at the side of the pot. If it comes out clean the plant needs watering.

Winter flower displays

At one time I used to preserve foliage to use in winter flower displays. Pick the mature foliage, as the young leaves wither more easily. Crush about 1 inch of the stem and leave overnight or longer in water. Next put one part glycerine and two parts hot water in a jug and stand the branches in the solution until they have absorbed it all or have changed colour. If moisture appears on the leaves, remove them from the solution. This process usually takes from one to two weeks. Do not use foliage that has started to change to autumn colouring as this will only wither. Cooper beech used to be my favourite foliage to preserve.

It's well worth picking leaves and bracken of all types. Press between sheets of newspapers and place under carpets. You will get some nice colour when fresh foliage is in short supply.

JUDGING HOME-MADE WINES

At many of the horticultural and agricultural shows there is a wine section - hundreds of bottles with all shades of wine fill the table.

A very small money prize, say 50p or so, may be awarded, or perhaps a certificate. Nonetheless, the competition is keen. There are rules for the competition but a good deal depends on the personal taste of the judge. Here's how to judge home-made wine and a few hints on how to exhibit it.

Make sure you read the schedule.

Make sure that you have all the equipment you will need for judging:-

corkscrew, glasses for tasting, a spittoon (pail), bowl for washing glasses, glass cloth, dry biscuits or bread, pen or pencil, marking sheet and a show schedule.

Standard to look for:
(a) presentation,
(b) clarity,
(c) colour,
(d) aroma and bouquet,
(e) flavour, balance and quality.

When exhibiting:
Make sure the wine is in the right class.
Make sure that it is presented in the correct type of bottle. For show purposes the bottle should be of clear glass.
The bottle should be filled so that when the cork is pushed right home the air space in the neck of the bottle is about 1" from the bottom of the cork.
Only corks with flanged heads should be used.
The label should be according to type or ingredients. A stick-on label should be 2" above the bottom edge.

Wine Making Tips.
I don't think people realise the power of home made wine. I use to make over 80 gallons (over 450 bottles!) a year. We had some good cheese and home made wine parties at my old home in Charsfield. so many happy evenings and bad hangovers next day!
I still make a little Elderflower wine. This is one of the best. Remember to pick the flowers in dry weather. Always make a note of the ingredients and tie to the handle of the demijohn, so that you can repeat (or improve on) the brew next time.
The beauty of wine making is that you can make a good drop of wine from so many fruit and vegetables even cartons of fruit juice if you have no fresh - but I always say "the countryside gives us so much and its all free!"

Cloudy
I often get asked why is this wine cloudy? I get two egg shells and bake them in a slow oven until they are dry and crumble easily. Put one teaspoon of crumbled eggshell into 1 gallon of cloudy wine and

leave for a few weeks. You will be surprised! Now siphon off the wine carefully, leaving the sediment at the bottom. I have also used 2 cubes of lemon jelly, melted in a little hot water and this will often clear the wine.

Dandelion
Do not pick from the roadside, as all the car fumes etc get on them, Also make sure no agricultural sprays have been used on them.

Elderberry Rob
I still get phone calls each year asking how to make 'Elderberry Rob', the old cure for sore throats and colds. All you needs 1lb. (400grams) of crushed fresh Elderberries, 1 lb. brown sugar. Simmer the fruit with the sugar until the consistancy of syrup. Sieve and bottle, ready for use in the winter months. Blackberry syrup can be made in the same way. These are a must for every medicine cabinet! Any wine left in the bottle can be frozen in ice cube trays to be used in cooking when needed.

Liqueurs

When making Raspberry Brandy dont throw the fruit away. Make a trifle, filling the sponge with fruit. When making Sloe, Damson or Bullace Gin, after straining put the fruit in a cheap sherry for a few weeks. You will get a good kick out of the sherry. When making Peach wine use the strained fruit for chutney. "Waste not, want not" my mother always said.

Parsnip

The most popular country wine years ago. It can be very powerful!. I have added about 1lb of rose hips (after a frost) to give wine a rich autumn glow.

Sugar

I never put all the sugar in that the recipes suggests as sometimes wine would be too sweet. You can always add a little sugar syrup in later.

A FEW TALES

GOBSTOPPERS

Jim was taking up his potatoes, a rather poor crop, watched by the village know-all, Joe by name.

"Rare lot o' littluns yar got there Jim bor."

"I know they are" answered Jim testily, "I grewed em to fit my mouth, not yars."

CARROTS

Not far from Ipswich, in a large and busy village, lived an old smallholder named Arthur who could scarcely be described as `something in the City', yet his business instincts and methods were keen and very much to the point.

On his gate one morning appeared a large notice with the announcement: "Karrits sold here: 6p bunch."

Many people remarked on his example of phonetic spelling and old

Arthur's lack of education.

One day, an acquaintance pointed out his error in spelling. Arthur smiled in his sly way. "I'm well aware of that" he replied "but if I spelt it the right way noone would take a scrap of notice."

TINNED PEAS

An old lady asked her husband to go into the garden and cut a cabbage for dinner. As he seemed a long time, she went to see what was wrong and found him lying dead among the vegetables. Later, telling her neighbour about this: "Oh, you poor thing," full of sympathy the neighbour said, "Whatever did you do?"

"Well" she replied, "I went and opened a tin of peas."

GOOD RHUBARB

A certain old lady who lived in a Suffolk village gave the lady of the village some rhubarb, which she had been growing in her garden. As she gave it to the lady she said "My dear, that old rhubarb ean't half so gud as it wuz, cuz it don't get no liquid manure now. I've got flush toilets."

NOT SO DAFT
At the Mental Hospital, one of the patients was walking in the garden, and met the gardener with a barrow loaded with farmyard manure.
"What are you going to do with that?" asked the patient.
"I'm going to put it on my strawberries" was the gardener's reply.
"Oh" said the patient, "I put sugar on mine."